TRADITIONAL
CROSS STITCH

TRADITIONAL
CROSS STITCH
A COLLECTION OF INSPIRATIONAL PROJECTS

DOROTHY WOOD

Photographs by Lucy Mason

HERMES HOUSE

This edition published in the UK in 1997 by Hermes House

This edition published in Canada by Book Express,
a division of Raincoast Books, 8680 Cambie Street,
Vancouver, British Columbia V6P 6M9

© 1997 Anness Publishing Limited

Hermes House is an imprint of
Anness Publishing Limited
Hermes House
88-89 Blackfriars Road
London SE1 8HA

ISBN 1-901289-97-4

Publisher: Joanna Lorenz
Project Editor: Joanne Rippin
Designer: Janet James
Photographer: Lucy Mason
Charts: Ethan Danielson

This book has previously been published as part of a larger compendium,
The Ultimate Cross Stitch Companion

Printed and bound in Hong Kong

1 3 5 7 9 10 8 6 4 2

CONTENTS

THREADS

Although stranded cotton is probably the most popular and versatile thread for cross stitch embroidery, there is an amazing range of different threads available.

Coton perlé produces attractive raised stitches and tapestry wool makes big, chunky cross stitches on a seven or eight count canvas. Some of the projects in this book use other familiar threads such as coton à broder or soft cotton but many are worked in new threads such as silky Marlitt or the more rustic flower thread which is ideal for stitching on linen. New threads are appearing on the market all the time. Look out for unusual flower threads which have been dyed in shaded natural colours and metallic threads which have been specially made for cross stitching.

TAPESTRY WOOL

Although traditionally associated with needlepoint, tapestry wool is also suitable for some cross stitch. It is usually worked on a chunky seven count canvas and makes a warm, hard-wearing cover for cushions, stools and chairs.

FLOWER THREAD OR NORDIN

This rustic cotton thread is ideal for working on evenweave linen fabrics. In thickness it is equivalent to two or three strands of stranded cotton. It is available in solid colours, but look out for the space-dyed skeins.

MARLITT

A lustrous rayon thread, Marlitt has been introduced to provide the sheen and beauty of silk at an economical price. Although only available in solid colours, it has four strands, allowing the colours to be mixed "in the needle".

COTON PERLÉ

This twisted thread has a distinct pearly sheen and is available in over 300 different colours. It comes in several different thicknesses and is generally used to produce a slightly raised effect on a variety of fabrics.

STRANDED COTTON

This is the most popular embroidery thread and is available in over 400 different colours. It is a versatile thread which can be divided into six separate strands. The separated strands of several colours can be intermingled to create a mottled effect when stitched.

METALLIC THREADS

Although traditionally unsuitable for cross stitch embroidery, some metallic threads are now specially made to sew through fabric. They are available in a range of colours as well as gold and silver. Finer metallic threads known as blending filaments can be worked together with strands of embroidery thread to add an attractive sparkle or sheen.

FABRICS

Evenweave fabrics have the same number of threads running in each direction. The number of threads in each 2½ cm (1 in) of fabric determines the gauge or "count". The larger the number of threads, the finer the fabric. Aida and Hardanger are woven and measured in blocks of threads. However, cross stitches worked on 28 count linen are the same size as those on 14 count Aida because the stitches are worked over two threads of linen.

LINEN

Traditionally pure linen was used, but there are now several different mixed fibre evenweave fabrics in a wide range of colours.

AIDA AND HARDANGER

These popular fabrics have groups of threads woven together to produce distinctive blocks over which the embroidery is worked.

   Aida comes in 8–18 count whereas Hardanger is a 22 count fabric. It can be used for fine stitching or worked as an 11 count fabric.

EVENWEAVE BANDS

Aida or evenweave bands come in a variety of widths. Some are plain and others have decorative edges. Once stitched, these bands can be applied to a background fabric or made up into bows, tie-backs or bags.

FANCY WEAVES

Fabrics specially woven with distinct areas for cross stitching are suitable for making into napkins, tablecloths and cot covers. There are also some unusual evenweaves which have linen or Lurex threads interwoven into the fabric for special effects.

CANVAS

Double and single thread canvas is usually associated with needlepoint but can be used successfully for cross stitch embroidery. Wool and coton perlé are particularly suitable threads for using when stitching on canvas.

WASTE CANVAS

A non-interlocked canvas is used to work cross stitch on non-evenweave fabric or ready-made items. It is specially made so that it can be frayed and removed after the cross stitch is worked.

NON-FRAY FABRICS

Plastic canvas, vinyl weave and stitching paper are all used for cross stitch projects where it is important that the fabric should not fray.

ADDITIONAL FABRICS

Iron-on interfacing is sometimes used to provide a backing for the cross stitch design.

   Fusible bonding web is generally used for appliqué.

1: linens; 2: plastic canvas, stitching paper, fusible bonding web, iron-on interfacing; 3: aida and linen bands; 4: 14 and 10 count waste canvas; 5: aida and white Hardanger; 6: canvases; 7: fancy weaves.

1

2

3

4

5

6

7

TECHNIQUES:BEGINNING

PREPARING THE FABRIC

Many of the projects in this book use evenweave fabrics which tend to fray easily, therefore it is advisable to finish the edges before starting the embroidery. An allowance has been made for neatening the edges in calculating the materials needed.

MASKING TAPE

A quick method for projects worked on inter-locking bar frames. The tape can be stapled or pinned to a frame.

ZIGZAG

Machine-stitched zigzag is used when embroidering parts of a garment since the seams will be neatened ready to stitch together.

BLANKET STITCH

This is the best all round method of neatening evenweave fabric. Either turn a small hem or stitch round the raw edge.

LEFT TO RIGHT: masking tape, zigzag and blanket stitch.

COVERING A HOOP

Embroidery hoops (frames) have two rings, one is solid and the other has a screw-fastening. The fabric is sandwiched between the two rings and the screw-fastening adjusted to keep the fabric taut. In order to protect the fabric and stitches from damage, the inner ring is wrapped with narrow cotton tape. Remember that some delicate fabrics can be damaged in an embroidery hoop (frame). In these cases it is advisable to use a large hoop which extends beyond the cross stitch area. Interlocking bar frames are ideal for small projects and a rotating frame is best for large pieces of work.

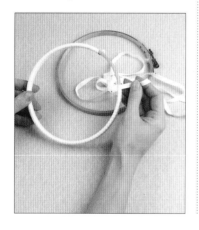

STARTING & FINISHING THREADS

There are several ways to begin a piece of cross stitch. Finish by sliding the needle under several stitches and trimming the end.

1 Fold a length of cotton in half and thread into the needle. Work the first half of the cross stitch, then thread the needle through the loop on the reverse side.

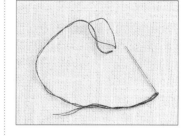

2 Leave a length of 5 cm (2 in) thread at the back of the fabric and weave this in when you have worked a block of stitches.

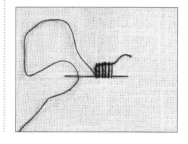

WASTE CANVAS

This technique allows charted cross stitch to be worked on non-evenweave fabric or ready-made items such as towels and cushions. Waste canvas is specially made so that the threads can be easily removed. It is only available in 10 and 14 count but you could use ordinary canvas provided that the threads are not interlocked.

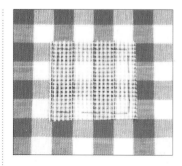

1 Tack (baste) a piece of canvas onto the area to be stitched. Make sure there will be plenty of canvas round the design once it is complete.

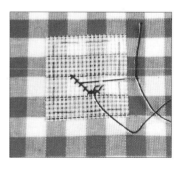

2 Work the cross stitch design over the canvas and through the fabric. Take care to make all the stitches as even as you possibly can.

3 Once complete, fray the canvas and pull the threads out one at a time. It will be easier if you tug the canvas gently to loosen the threads.

TECHNIQUES:FINISHING

MITRED CORNER

Tablecloths and mats can be finished neatly with mitred corners. These reduce bulk and make a secure hem which can be laundered safely.

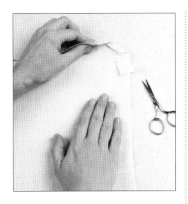 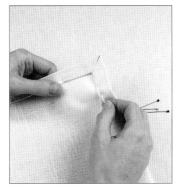

1 Fold the hem, run your fingers along and open out. Cut across the corner from crease to crease and refold the hem.

2 Turn under a further 0.5 cm (1/4 in) and pin the hem in place. Slip stitch the mitred corner and machine or hand stitch the hem.

STRETCHING

As a general rule embroidery should always be stretched using thread so that it can be easily removed and cleaned in the future. However, small projects which may be kept for only a limited time can be quickly and successfully mounted using double-sided tape.

1 Cut the card (cardboard) to the required size and stick double-sided tape along all the edges. Trim across the corners and remove the paper backing. Stretch the fabric onto the tape and mitre the corners neatly.

MOUNTING

If a project such as a sampler or picture is likely to be kept for a long time, great care should be taken in mounting the finished work. Acid-free mount board (backing board) or paper should be used under the embroidery and glue or tape which leave an acid residue on the fabric should be avoided.

The following easy method of mounting ensures that the embroidery will be absolutely straight and exactly where you want it.

1 Cut the mount board to size and mark the mid point across the top and bottom of the board. Allow for a wider border at the bottom if required. Mark the mid point of the embroidery at each side of the board and draw in the lines. Lay the embroidery face down on a flat surface and place the mount board on top of it.

2 Line up the guide-lines on the embroidery with the lines on the board. Fold the top edge over and put a pin into the mount board at the centre line. Stretch the fabric slightly and put another pin at the bottom. Repeat the process at the sides. Work your way along each edge from the centre out putting in pins every 2.5 cm (1 in) keeping the grain of the fabric straight.

3 Using a long length of double thread, sew from side to side spacing the stitches about 12 mm (1/2 in) apart. Join in more thread using an overhand knot. Once complete lift the threads up one at a time to pull them tight and secure. Mitre or fold the corners and repeat along the remaining sides.

ADDITIONS

Most embroidery is embellished by the addition of trimmings, and cross stitch is no exception. Whether it is an Asian design with shisha mirrors and tassels or a traditional English lavender bag edged with Victorian lace, the "additions" always enhance the cross stitch design and add the finishing touch to an attractive piece.

BEADS

Beads are attached using a double thread and in contrast to all other forms of embroidery, begun with a securely tied knot. Sew the beads on individually, as if you were stitching the first half of a cross stitch.

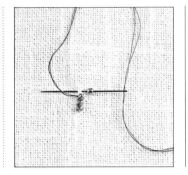

BUTTONS

Buttons with four holes can be stitched on with a large cross stitch to make a very attractive addition to a design.

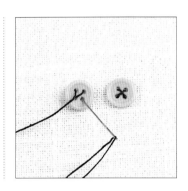

RIBBON

Ribbon looks very effective when used to create a grid for a repeat design of small cross stitch motifs. The ribbon is laid straight along the grain before the cross stitch has been worked. Choose a ribbon which is the same width as one cross stitch. If the ribbon is to be applied diagonally it is easier to work the cross stitch motifs first.

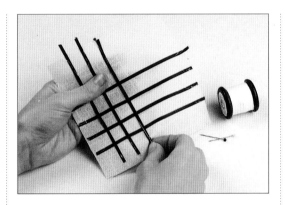

1 Pin the strips of ribbon in position in one direction and pin the rest across the top. Check that the spacing is correct, then tack the ends.

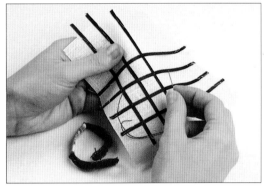

2 Sew a cross stitch at each junction where the ribbons overlap. Remember that if the ribbons are applied diagonally, the cross stitch will be upright.

MAKING A CORD

Embroidery threads are ideal for making into fine cord. The threads can be all one colour or mixed colours to match each particular project.

The amount of thread you need depends on the final thickness of the cord required. As a rough guide, a 1 m (39 in) length of threads ready to twist will make a cord about 40 cm (16 in) long.

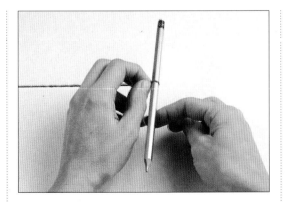

1 Cut several lengths of thread, two and a half times the final cord length. Fix one end to a secure point. Slip a pencil through the threads at the other end and twist the pencil like a propeller.

2 Keep turning until the cord begins to twist together. Hold the middle of the cord and bring the ends together. Smooth any kinks with your fingers and tie the ends with an overhand knot.

SHISHA MIRROR

These irregular pieces of mirror are stitched on to garments and hangings as a protection against evil. If spirits see themselves reflected in the mirror then, it is believed, they will flee.

Traditional shisha mirrors can be bought from ethnic suppliers, but large modern sequins are a suitable alternative. As extra security, stick the mirror or sequins in position using a small piece of double-sided tape or a dab of glue.

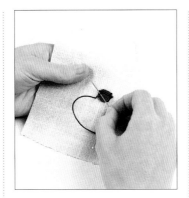

1 Sew two threads across the shisha from top to bottom. Sew across the shisha in the other direction looping the thread round each laid thread to create a framework.

2 Bring the needle up close to the shisha, make a loop through the framework, cross over the loop and pull the thread gently towards you. Take the needle back to the reverse side.

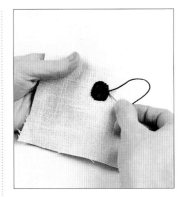

3 Continue round the shisha beginning each stitch between the ends of the previous loop. Finish the thread off on the reverse side.

MAKING TASSELS

One of the prettiest ways to complete a project is to make your own tassels from threads which were used in the embroidery. There are many different ways to make tassels, but most use the same basic technique.

The two following methods are both easy to make. The first tassel is ideal for stitching on to the corners of cushions, mats or bookmarks whereas the second is worked over the end of a cord or rouleau and produces a very professional result. Make the tassels more ornate by adding beads or stitching rows of interlocking blanket stitch round the head until it is completely covered.

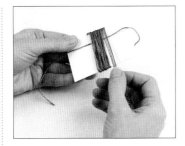

1 Cut a piece of card (cardboard) slightly deeper than the finished length of the tassel. Wind threads round the card as required and slip a length of thread underneath.

2 Cut along the bottom of the threads and tie the bundle together using a sailor's knot. This is like a reef knot, but the thread is twisted round twice before pulling it tight.

3 Wrap another length of thread round the tassel to form a neck and tie off as before. Trim the ends neatly.

1 Wind threads round the card (cardboard) and cut along one side. Tie a knot near the end of the cord or rouleau and place it in the middle of the bundle of threads.

2 Enclose the knot with the threads and tie a separate length of thread around just above the knot.

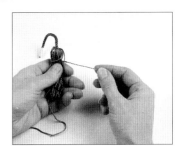

3 Hold the cord and bring all the threads down together. Wrap a length of cord round underneath the knot and tie off securely as before. Trim the tassel ends neatly.

NIGHTDRESS CASE

Match the ribbon in the white crocheted lace edging to the brilliant blue of these pretty cornflowers and bow.

YOU WILL NEED

1.5 m (1²/₃ yd) white cotton fabric

10 x 13 cm (4 x 5 in) 12 count waste canvas

tacking (basting) thread

needle

embroidery hoop (frame)

stranded cotton DMC 798, 799, 3347

embroidery needle

tailor's chalk

sewing machine

sewing thread

scissors

60 cm (24 in) white crocheted lace with ribbon insert

pins

WORKING THE CROSS STITCH

Tack (baste) the waste canvas in the centre of the cotton fabric 10 cm (4 in) from one end. Work the cross stitch through the waste canvas using two strands of cotton. The bow should be at the end of the fabric. Manipulate the canvas to loosen the threads and pull them out one by one. Press the embroidery on the reverse side.

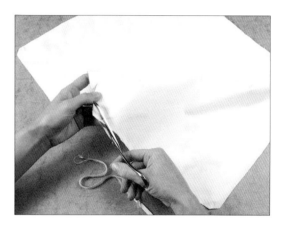

1 To make up: fold the fabric in half crossways and mark the triangular flap with tailor's chalk. With right sides together, stitch round the edge, leaving a gap on one side. Trim the seams and cut across the corners before turning through.

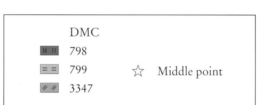

DMC	
▦▦	798
═ ═	799 ☆ Middle point
⁄⁄ ⁄⁄	3347

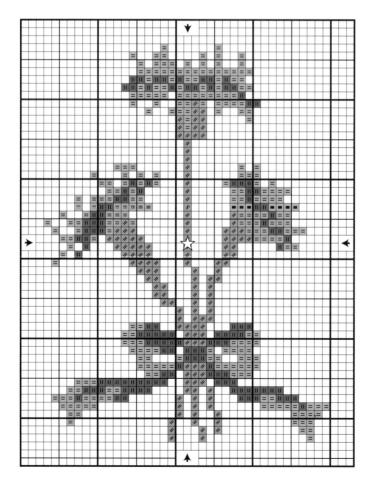

2 Ease out the corners and point of the flap and press on the reverse side. Pin and tack the lace along the edge of the flap and stitch it in place. Fold in the ends of the lace and hand sew. Slip stitch the side seams to finish.

TABLECLOTH AND NAPKIN

This pretty table linen set with its colourful border will make Sunday lunch a very elegant affair.

YOU WILL NEED

115 cm (45 in) square of white 28 count Jobelan for the tablecloth

50 cm (20 in) square of white 28 count Jobelan for the napkin

tacking (basting) thread

scissors

needle

embroidery hoop (frame)

stranded cotton Anchor 3 skeins each of 131 and 133, 1 skein each of 35, 47, 110, 112, 211, 297

tapestry needle

pins

sewing thread

sewing machine

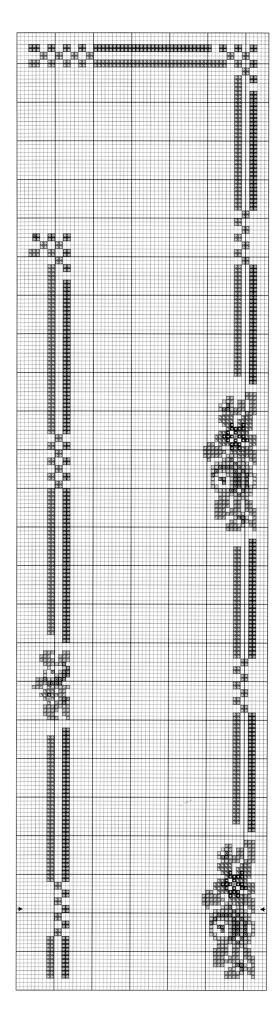

TABLECLOTH

WORKING THE CROSS STITCH

Fold the fabric in half and tack (baste) a guideline about 20 cm (8 in) along one fold to mark the centre on each side. Tack a line across one of these sides, 16 cm (6¼ in) from the edge, as a starting-point. Work the cross stitch using two strands of cotton over two threads.

1 To make up: the chart shows one half of one side. Repeat the design on the other side, keeping the floral motifs facing in the same direction. Continue the cross stitch round the other sides of the tablecloth.

2 Press on the wrong side of the fabric when finished. Trim the fabric to a 95 cm (37½ in) square, mitre the corners and fold over a 2.5 cm (1 in) hem. Stitch close to the turned edge and slip stitch the mitred corners.

NAPKIN

WORKING THE CROSS STITCH

Tack (baste) the centre line as before and mark the starting point 8 cm (3 in) in from the side. Work the cross stitch using two strands of cotton over two threads, repeating the design on all sides.

1 To make up: press the fabric on the reverse side when complete and trim to 45 cm (18 in).

Mitre the corners and fold over a 2 cm (¾ in) hem. Finish in the same way as the tablecloth.

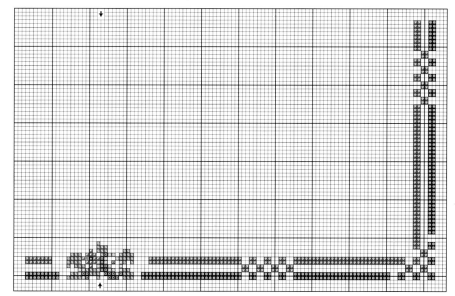

Anchor			
⑂⑂	297	∅∅	211
∞∞	133	◀◀	112
◈◈	131	◥◥	110
▫▫	47		
⊞⊞	35		

FLORAL TIEBACKS

These tiebacks are quick and easy to make and are ideal for the kitchen or utility room.

YOU WILL NEED

*1.5 m (1⅔ yd) of
8 cm (3 in) raw linen band,
Zweigart E7272*

scissors

tacking (basting) thread

needle

tapestry needle

*stranded cotton DMC 517, 518,
553, 554, 561, 562, 563, 741*

pins

four 2.5 cm (1 in) brass rings

WORKING THE CROSS STITCH

Cut the linen band into four equal pieces. Tack (baste) guidelines across one of the bands to mark the centre and work the cross stitch using two strands of cotton over two threads. Turn the band round and repeat the design at the other end.

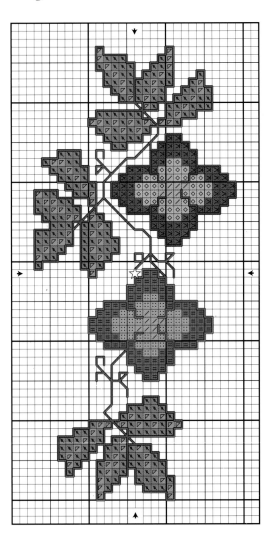

DMC	
▬▬	517
⋮⋮⋮	518
▷▷	553
◇◇	554
◣◣	562
▽▽	563
⁄⁄	741

Backstitch	
▬▬	561
▬▬	553
▬▬	517

☆ Middle point

1 To make up: press the band on the reverse side and fold over 5 mm (¼ in) at each end. Fold in the corners to make a point, then pin and tack. Finish a plain piece of linen band in the same way: this will form the backing.

2 Pin the tieback and its facing together, with the raw edges to the inside. Sew a decorative cross stitch every 1 cm (½ in) along the border to join the two pieces together. Slip a brass ring between the layers at each point and sew cross stitches on the point and at either side to secure. Make a second matching tieback in exactly the same way.

HERB BOX AND POT STAND

YOU WILL NEED

*60 cm (24 in) of 10 cm (4 in)
wide plain bleached linen,
Inglestone collection 900/100*

tacking (basting) thread

needle

*stranded cotton DMC white,
210, 211, 300, 310, 311, 318,
340, 349, 445, 472, 500,
562, 704, 726, 741, 742, 809,
966, 3607, 3746*

tapestry needle

scissors

30 cm (12 in) pinewood box

staple gun

*Keep the herb box on the windowsill filled with fresh herbs. The special
heatproof glass inside the pot stand frame will protect the design.*

HERB BOX

WORKING THE CROSS STITCH

Tack (baste) guidelines across
the centre of the linen band in
both directions then work the
cross stitch design using two
strands of cotton over two
threads of the linen.

1 To make up: once complete, press
the linen on the wrong side and then
fit round the box. Turn under the ends
and staple them to the back of the box.

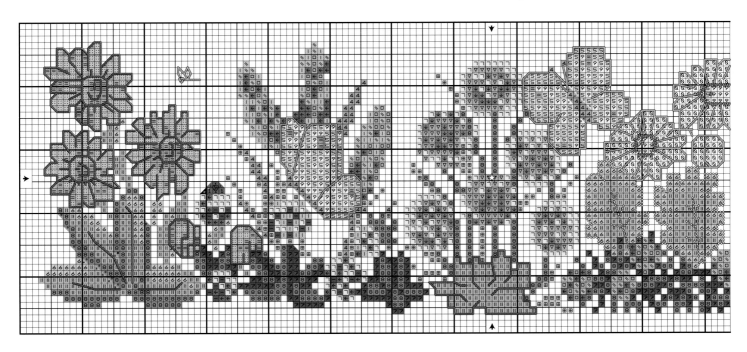

POT STAND

YOU WILL NEED

*23 cm (9 in) square of white
18 count Aida*

tacking (basting) thread

needle

scissors

tapestry needle

embroidery hoop (frame)

*stranded cotton
Anchor 120, 122*

*hexagonal frame,
Framecraft WTS*

DMC		DMC	
⟍⟍	210	▢▢	809
⊐⊐	211	⊞⊞	966
▬▬	311	↓↓	3607
I I	340	←←	3746
▪▪	349	◎◎	white
22	310	▽▽	3607 +211
◨◨	300		(1 strand each)
44	318		Backstitch
55	445	——	500
66	472	—♥	300
77	500	—	472
88	562	∘∘∘∘	966
99	726	—♦	318
II II	704	——	310
==	741		
⋮⋮	742	☆	Middle point

WORKING THE CROSS STITCH

Tack (baste) guidelines across the centre of the Aida in both directions. Work the cross stitch using two strands of cotton. Sew the backstitch outlines and press the work on the wrong side. Follow the manufacturer's instructions to fit the embroidery inside the frame. The pot stand has a felt base to protect tables.

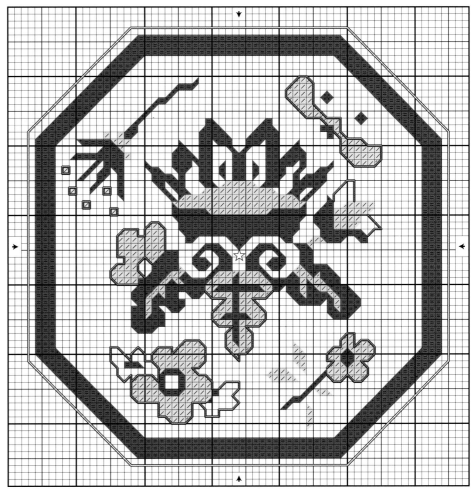

Anchor (in two strands)		Backstitch (in one strand)	Backstitch (in two strands)	
▬▬	122	—— 122	——	120
⟋⟋	120		☆	Middle point

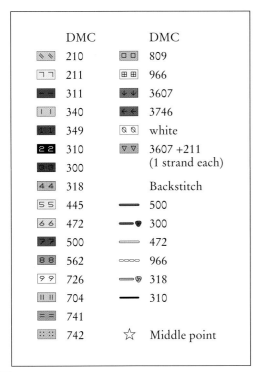

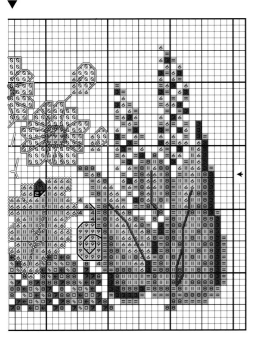

TRADITIONAL

EMBROIDERED SHEET AND PILLOW CASE

This classic bed linen would look superb with a Victorian blue and white wash bowl and jug set on a marble washstand.

YOU WILL NEED

8 cm (3 in) wide Aida band, Fabric Flair BA7349

scissors

sheet and pillow case

stranded cotton Anchor pillow case - two skeins of 130, 132 and one of 134 single sheet - six skeins of 130, five of 132 and three of 134

tapestry needle

pins

sewing thread

sewing machine

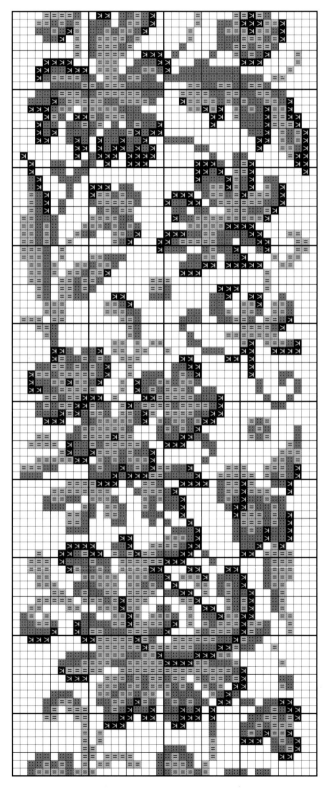

WORKING THE CROSS STITCH

Measure the widths of the sheet and pillow case and cut the Aida band 10 cm (4 in) longer. Work the cross stitch design using two strands of cotton, beginning 5 cm (2 in) from one end.

1 To make up: once complete, press on the wrong side and pin to the sheet or pillow case 6 cm (2½ in) in from the edge. Turn under the ends and stitch the band in place.

Anchor

≡≡	130
▨	132
▶▶	134

SPOT MOTIF SAMPLER

Birds, butterflies and flowers were very popular motifs in the nineteenth century, but the pillars make this sampler quite unusual.

YOU WILL NEED

25 cm (10 in) square of Antique Aida 27 count Linda, Zweigart E1235

tacking (basting) thread

needle

embroidery hoop (frame)

stranded cotton Anchor 10, 303, 337, 352, 681, 844, 848, 884

tapestry needle

27 x 30 cm (10½ x 12 in) mount board (backing board)

strong thread

picture frame

WORKING THE CROSS STITCH

Tack (baste) guidelines across the centre of the linen in both directions. Work the cross stitch design using two strands of cotton over two threads.

1 To make up: press the embroidery on the reverse side when complete. Stretch the embroidery over the mount board (backing board) and fit into a picture frame of your choice.

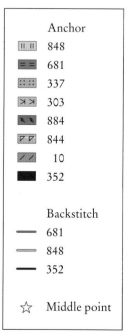

Anchor	
‖ ‖	848
= =	681
⋮⋮⋮	337
⤨⤨	303
◣◣	884
▽▽	844
╱╱	10
■	352

Backstitch	
—	681
—	848
—	352

☆ Middle point

EMBROIDERED COATHANGER

Protect delicate silk negligées and soft woollen sweaters with this pretty padded coathanger.

YOU WILL NEED

30 x 60 cm (12 x 24 in) fabric for the cover

scissors

5 x 25 cm (2 x 10 in) 10 count waste canvas

pins

tacking (basting) thread

needle

stranded cotton Anchor 19, 35, 118, 218, 302, 304

embroidery needle

30 cm (12 in) polyester wadding (batting)

wooden coathanger

sewing thread

double-sided tape

50 cm (20 in) fine cord

WORKING THE CROSS STITCH

Cut the fabric for the cover in half lengthways and the waste canvas into five equal pieces. Pin and tack (baste) a square of waste canvas in the middle of the fabric. Position the other pieces of canvas on either side, leaving a gap of 4 cm (1½ in) between them, and tack securely. Work the cross stitch using two strands of cotton. Once complete, loosen the threads of the waste canvas and pull them out one at a time. Press on reverse side.

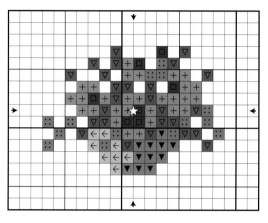

	Anchor		Anchor
⋮⋮	118	←	302
+	35	▽	218
⊡	19		
▼	304	☆	Middle point

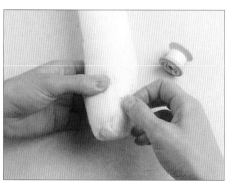

1 To make up: cut the wadding (batting) into four 5 cm (2 in) strips and one of 10 cm (4 in). Wrap the narrow bands round the coathanger and finish with the wider band. Oversew the ends.

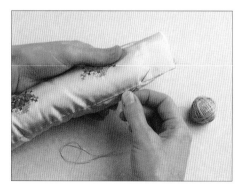

2 Trim both pieces of fabric to a width of 11 cm (4½ in), making sure that the cross stitch motifs are along the centre line. With right sides facing and a seam allowance of 1.5 cm (⅝ in), stitch the pieces together, leaving a small gap in the middle for the hook. Press the seam flat and place over the coathanger, feeding the hook through the gap. Turn under the front edge of the fabric, overlap at the bottom of the coathanger and slip stitch.

3 Fold in the fabric at the end of the coathanger and sew tiny running stitches close to the edge. Gather up the stitches and sew in to secure. Cover the hook with double-sided tape. Starting at the curved end, wrap the cord tightly round the hook and sew the end into the wadding of the coathanger to finish.

VICTORIAN SEWING SET

Keep your needles, pins and scissors handy in this pretty sewing set.

YOU WILL NEED

*36 x 46 cm (14 x 18 in)
cream 22 count Hardanger,
Zweigart E1008*

scissors

tacking (basting) thread

needle

interlocking bar frame

tapestry needle

*stranded cotton DMC 340, 341,
3685*

pins

sewing thread

*4.5 m (5 yd) of 3 mm (¹⁄8 in)
wine coloured ribbon*

*9 x 25 cm (3¹⁄2 x 10 in)
heavyweight iron-on interfacing*

*12 x 28 cm (4³⁄4 x 11 in) wine
coloured lining fabric*

8 x 24 cm (3 x 9¹⁄2 in) felt

*25 cm (10 in) thin card
(cardboard)*

all-purpose glue

NEEDLECASE

WORKING THE CROSS STITCH

Cut a piece of Hardanger 18 x 25 cm (7 x 10 in) and tack (baste) guidelines across the centre in both directions. Leave ten pairs of threads clear on either side of the crossways centre line and work two panels of the cross stitch design. Work the cross stitch using two strands of cotton over one pair of threads. Once complete, pin and tack the ribbon in place between the stitches and sew a large cross stitch where they overlap.

1 To make up: press on the reverse side and iron on the interfacing. Trim the Hardanger and mitre the corners. Fold over the edges and press them flat.

2 Press under a 1 cm (³⁄8 in) turning all round the lining. Pin and slip stitch the lining to the inside of the needlecase. Fold the felt in half crossways and lay on top of the lining. Stitch down the fold line to complete the needlecase.

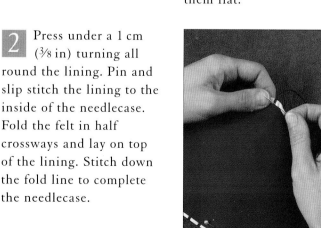

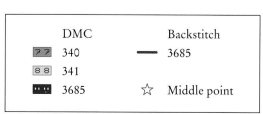

DMC		Backstitch	
⁊⁊	340	—	3685
88	341		
▪▪▪	3685	☆	Middle point

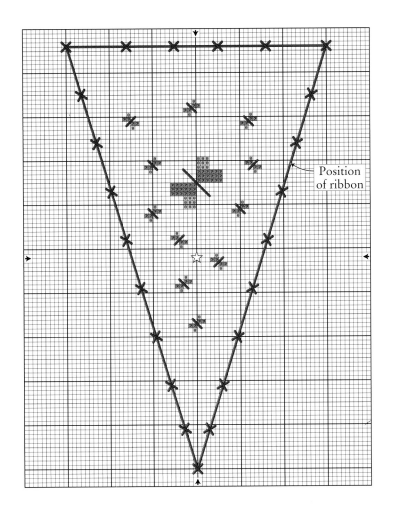

Position of ribbon

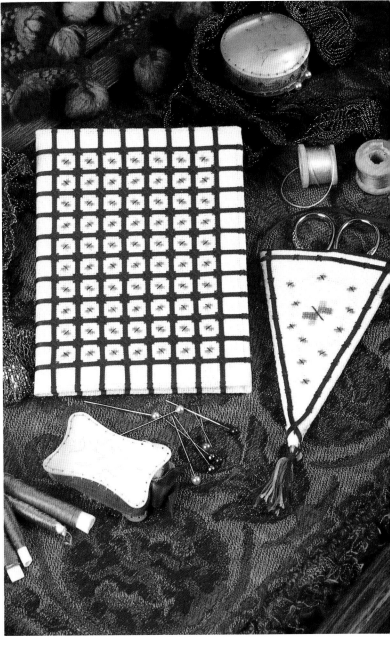

SCISSORS CASE

WORKING THE CROSS STITCH

Work two panels of the cross stitch design using two strands of cotton over one pair of threads. Press the embroidery on the reverse side when complete.

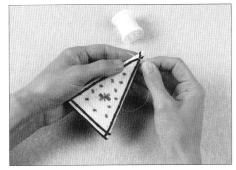

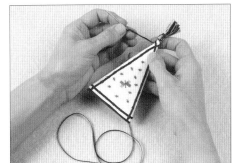

1 To make up: trace the template and cut four triangles from thin card (cardboard). Trim the seam allowance and, positioning the cross stitch carefully, stretch the Hardanger over the card using all-purpose glue. Cover the other two triangles with lining fabric.

2 Put the lining-covered pieces together with right sides facing and place an embroidered panel on either side with the lining protruding slightly at the top. Oversew the sides together securely.

3 Make a tassel by winding a length of stranded cotton round a 4 cm (1½ in) square of card (cardboard). Sew the strip of tassel onto the point and stitch a 70 cm (27½ in) length of ribbon to each side to finish.

SILK TOILET BAG

The design on this luxurious bag was inspired by the African violet, a flower much loved by the Victorians.

YOU WILL NEED

40 cm (16 in) of eyelet edge natural linen band, Inglestone Collection 979/50

stranded cotton DMC 341, 550, 744, 3746

tapestry needle

pins

35 x 40 cm (14 x 16 in) burgundy silk dupion (mid-weight silk)

sewing thread

sewing machine

25 x 40 cm (10 x 16 in) lining fabric

scissors

needle

six 12 mm (½ in) brass rings

1 m (1 yd) cream cord

WORKING THE CROSS STITCH

Fold the linen band in half lengthways and count the threads to find the centre of the band. Work the cross stitch using two strands of cotton over two threads of linen and repeat the design working out to each end.

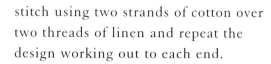

1 To make up: press on the reverse side, pin the band to the silk 10 cm (4 in) from the bottom edge and stitch close to the edges. With right sides together, stitch the lining to the silk along the top edge. Press the seam open and stitch the other edges together so that they make a tube shape.

2 Position the seam at the centre back and press open. Stitch along the bottom of the silk, trim and turn through. Turn in the seam allowance of the lining and slip stitch before tucking inside.

3 Cover the rings with buttonhole stitch. Stitch round the top of the bag along the seam line and space the rings evenly before stitching securely in place. Cut the cord in half. Thread the two pieces through in opposite directions and tie the ends together with overhand knots. Unravel the ends of the cord to make pretty tassels.

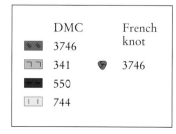

DMC		French knot
▨▨	3746	
⊓⊓	341	◈ 3746
▬	550	
⌶⌶	744	

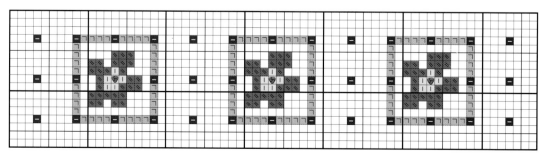

VICTORIAN CUSHION

TRADITIONAL

This design is adapted from some blue and white tiles which were very popular in Victorian times.

YOU WILL NEED

20 cm (8 in) square of Antique white 32 count Belfast linen, Zweigart E3609

tacking (basting) thread

needle

embroidery hoop (frame)

stranded cotton Anchor 1031, 1036

tapestry needle

scissors

50 cm (½ yd) of 90 cm (36 in) navy chintz

tailor's chalk

ruler

sewing machine

sewing thread

1.5 m (1⅔ yd) piping cord

36 cm (14 in) cushion pad

pins

WORKING THE CROSS STITCH

Tack (baste) guidelines across the centre of the linen in both directions and work the cross stitch using two strands of cotton over two threads. Turning the linen through 90 degrees each time, repeat the design in the other three quarters.

1 To make up: trim the linen to within 1.5 cm (⅝ in) of the cross stitch. Turn under 1 cm (³⁄₈ in), mitre the corners and press on the reverse side. Cut two 38 cm (15 in) squares of chintz. Pin and tack the panel in the centre of one piece and slip stitch securely. Draw out sufficient 5 cm (2 in) bias strips on the rest of the fabric to fit round the cushion. Join the bias strips, trim the seams and press open. Cover the piping cord with the strips and tack in place round the edge of the embroidered cushion panel. Stitch. Lay the other panel on top with right sides together and stitch around three sides. Insert the cushion pad and slip stitch the fourth side to complete.

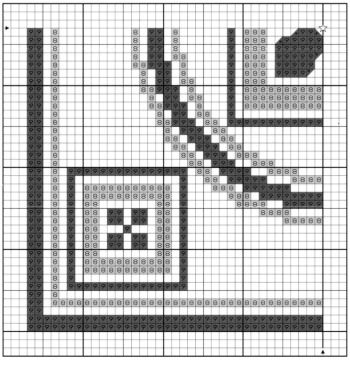

Anchor			
88	1032	99	1036	☆ Middle point

TOWEL BORDER

*These embroidered Arum lilies, commonly known as cuckoo pint,
look most attractive on a set of pale yellow towels.*

TRADITIONAL

WORKING THE CROSS STITCH

Tack (baste) guidelines in both directions across the centre of the cross stitch panel. Work the cross stitch using two strands of cotton and gold thread. Once complete work the leaf veins using a single strand and the outlines using two strands.

1 To finish: remove the tacking (basting) thread and press on the reverse side.

YOU WILL NEED

*white terry hand towel with
cross stitch border*

tacking (basting) thread

needle

embroidery hoop (frame)

scissors

*stranded cotton DMC 310,
680, 725, 727,
783, 895, 3346, 3362*

tapestry needle

gold thread DMC Art.284

	DMC
3 3	727
4 4	Art.284
⊥ ⊥	783
□ □	725
⊞ ⊞	895
↓ ↓	3362
⁄ ⁄	3346

	Backstitch
═══	680
▬▬▬	310
═══	895
☆	Middle point

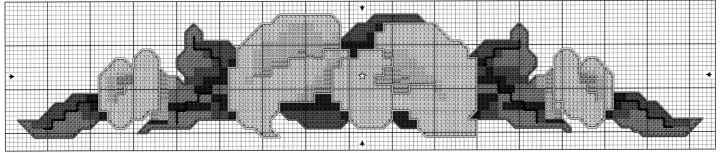

LAVENDER BAG

Tuck this little bag into a drawer to keep your clothes fresh and to remind you of late summer evenings and sweet-smelling flowers.

YOU WILL NEED

30 cm (12 in) of 7.5 cm (3 in) raw linen band with blue scalloped edges, Zweigart E7272

tacking (basting) thread

needle

coton perlé no. 8 DMC 208, 550, 780, 783, 907

tapestry needle

scissors

blue stranded cotton (thread) to match the scalloped edge

sewing thread

dried lavender flowers

WORKING THE CROSS STITCH

Tack (baste) a guideline lengthways down the centre of the band. Tack a second line crossways 6 cm (2½ in) from the top edge. Work the cross stitch over two threads and press on the reverse side.

1 To make up: press under 12 mm (½ in) on each raw edge of the band and sew two rows of running stitch using two strands of blue embroidery thread to secure.

2 Fold the band in half crossways and slip stitch the side seams. Fill with dried lavender flowers or pot pourri and slip stitch the top edges together.

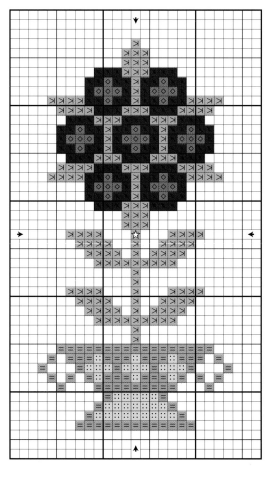

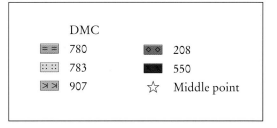

DMC		
☰ 780	◆	208
⦂⦂ 783	■	550
⊳⊳ 907	☆	Middle point

TABLE RUNNER

The linen for the runner is very fine, but the design is fairly quick to sew.

YOU WILL NEED

50 x 100 cm (20 x 40 in)
36 count white evenweave linen

tacking (basting) thread

needle

embroidery hoop (frame)

stranded cotton Anchor
six skeins of 391

tapestry needle

scissors

sewing machine

sewing thread

WORKING THE CROSS STITCH

Tack (baste) a guideline in one corner, 12 cm (4¾ in) in from each side. This marks the outside edge of the design. Work the cross stitch using two strands of cotton over three threads of the fabric. The second quarter of the design is a mirror image of the first and the second half of the design is a mirror image of the first half.

1 To make up: on completion of the stitching, press on the wrong side. Keeping an equal border all round the embroidery, trim the fabric to 40 x 88 cm (16 x 35 in). Mitre the corners and fold over a 2.5 cm (1 in) hem. Sew close to the fold and slip stitch the corners.

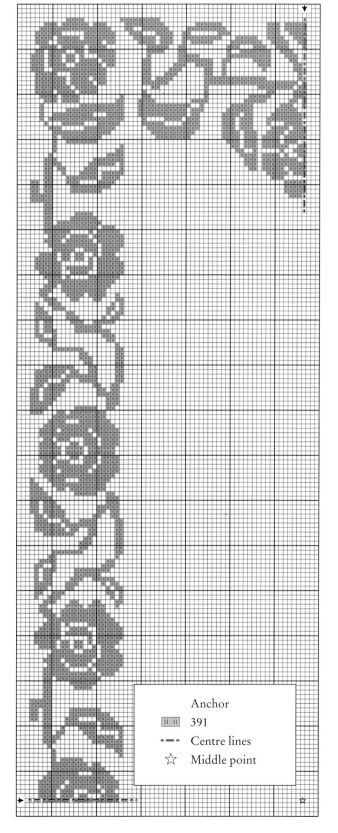

	Anchor
▦	391
– –	Centre lines
☆	Middle point

PICTURE MOUNT

Personalize the design by adding a name in the panel
below the photograph.

WORKING THE CROSS STITCH

Mark a 25 cm (10 in) square in the middle of the canvas and a second 10 cm (4 in) square in the centre of that one. Tack (baste) guidelines in the centre of each side of the "mount" and begin by stitching the bow. The second side is a mirror image of the first. Press the embroidery on the reverse side once complete.

1 To make up: cut out a 10 cm (4 in) square from the centre of the mount board (backing board) and stick double-sided tape round this edge. Cut into each corner of the centre square on the fabric and trim. Position the fabric under the mount and stretch gently onto the tape. Put more tape round the outside edge. Mitre the corners and stretch the fabric onto the tape, checking that the design is square. Fit into a frame of your choice.

YOU WILL NEED

35 cm (14 in) square 32 count
natural evenweave linen
safety ruler
tailor's chalk
tacking (basting) thread
needle
embroidery hoop (frame)
white stranded cotton
tapestry needle
scissors
25 cm (10 in) square of
mount board (backing board)
craft knife
double-sided tape
picture frame

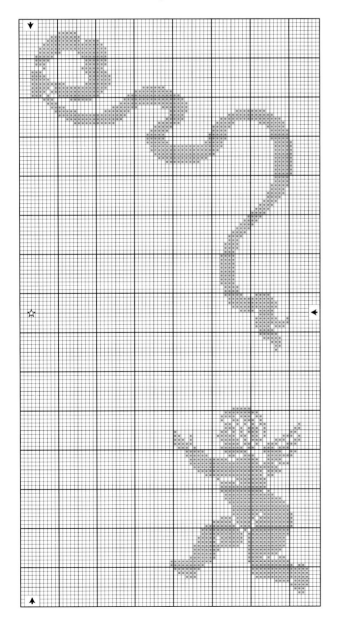

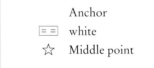

Anchor	
= =	white
☆	Middle point

JEWELLERY BOX

This Charles Rennie Mackintosh design could be adapted to fit any square or rectangular box you may have.

YOU WILL NEED

25 cm (10 in) square gold 32 count evenweave linen

tacking (basting) thread

needle

interlocking bar frame

tapestry needle

stranded cotton DMC ecru, 310, 645, 648

Anchor Marlitt 872

light gold thread DMC Art.282

gold thread Glissen gloss luster numbers 02 and 03

balger cord Kreinik 105C and 225C

scissors

double-sided tape

polyester wadding (batting)

wooden box

1 m (1 yd) of 15 mm (⅝ in) corded ribbon

WORKING THE CROSS STITCH

Tack (baste) guidelines in both directions across the centre of the linen. Work the cross stitch using two strands of cotton and single lengths of cable. Press the design on the reverse side when complete and trim to 3 cm (1¼ in) larger than the box.

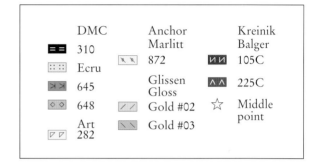

	DMC		Anchor Marlitt		Kreinik Balger
	310		872		105C
	Ecru		Glissen Gloss		225C
	645		Gold #02		Middle point
	648		Gold #03		
	Art 282				

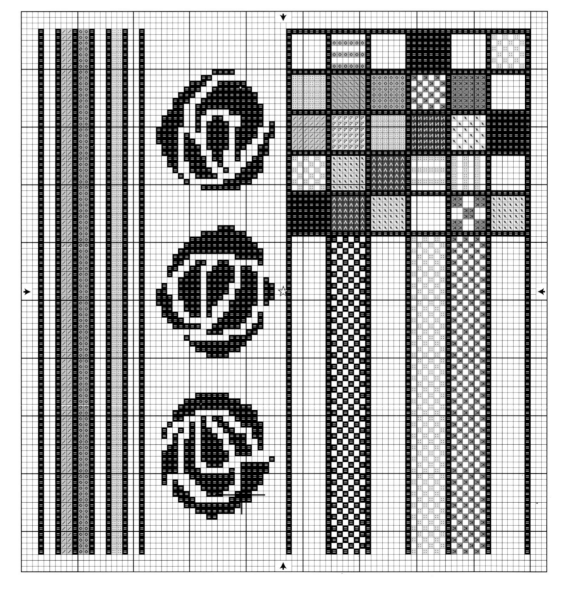

1 To make up: cut a
square of wadding
(batting) and stick it to the
lid of the box. Put double-
sided tape round the side
of the lid and stretch the
linen onto it, folding in
the corners neatly.

2 Put more double-
sided tape round the
side of the lid and stick the
ribbon down to cover the
raw edges. Fold over the
end and stick down.

FLORAL TRAY

This delightful tray has a glass inset to protect the embroidery.

YOU WILL NEED

30 cm (12 in) square of cream 28 count Cashel linen, Zweigart E3281

tacking (basting) thread

needle

embroidery hoop (frame)

stranded cotton DMC 347, 500, 646, 648, 918, 919, 948, 3047, 3768, 3815

tapestry needle

24 cm (9½ in) wooden tray, Framecraft WSST

strong thread

WORKING THE CROSS STITCH

Tack (baste) guidelines in both directions across the centre of the linen. Work the cross stitch using two strands of cotton and press on the reverse side when the design is complete.

1 To make up: stretch the embroidery over the supplied mount board (backing board) and assemble the tray according to the manufacturer's instructions.

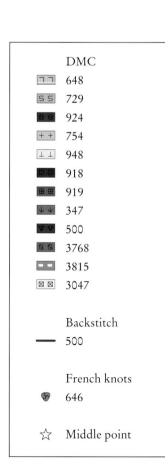

	DMC
7 7	648
5 5	729
8 8	924
+ +	754
⊥ ⊥	948
■ ■	918
⊞ ⊞	919
↓ ↓	347
▼ ▼	500
◎ ◎	3768
▬ ▬	3815
⊠ ⊠	3047

Backstitch

— 500

French knots

● 646

☆ Middle point

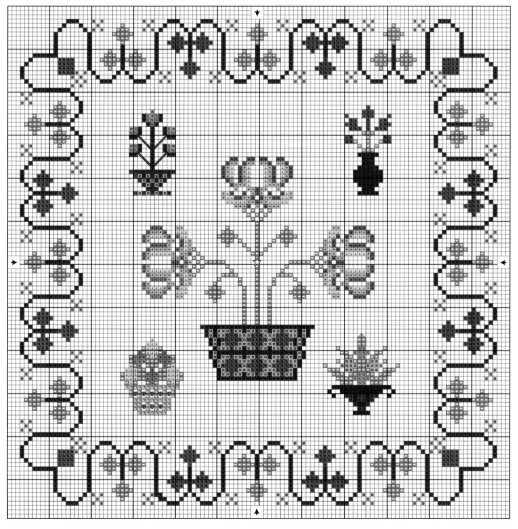

EMBROIDERED SLIPPERS

A plain pair of slippers can be made special with this pretty rose motif.

pair of black velvet slippers

*two 9 cm (3½ in) squares of
14 count waste canvas*

*Anchor Nordin 22, 35,
47, 244, 246, 306, 365, 9046*

tapestry needle

thimble

steam iron

WORKING THE CROSS STITCH

Position the waste canvas on the front of the first slipper and tack (baste) in place. Find the centre point of the canvas and begin stitching the design. The stitches are worked through the velvet only, using a thimble for ease.

1 To make up: the second slipper design is a mirror image of the first. When both are complete, pull the canvas threads out one at a time. Steam the front of the slippers to even out the stitches.

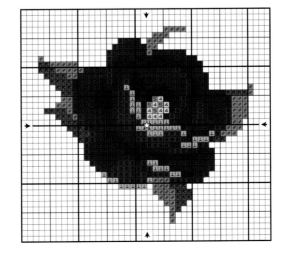

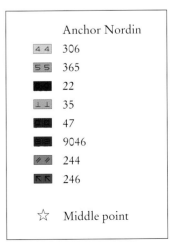

Anchor Nordin	
4 4	306
5 5	365
■	22
⊥ ⊥	35
■	47
▦	9046
⁄ ⁄	244
◤ ◤	246
☆	Middle point

PRAM QUILT

Children can learn basic colours and numbers using this cleverly designed bright and cheerful quilt.

YOU WILL NEED

61 cm x 76 cm (24 in x 30 in) Anne fabric, Zweigart E7563

embroidery hoop (frame)

stranded cotton DMC 310, 349, 550, 608, 700, 702, 741, 781, 783, 791, 793, 898, 972

tapestry needle

51 x 64 cm (20 x 25 in) medium weight iron-on interfacing

61 x 76 cm (24 x 30 in) cotton lining fabric

61 x 71 cm (24 x 28 in) 4oz wadding (batting)

pins

sewing machine

sewing thread

scissors

needle

3 m (3¼ yd) of 7 mm (¼ in) ribbon

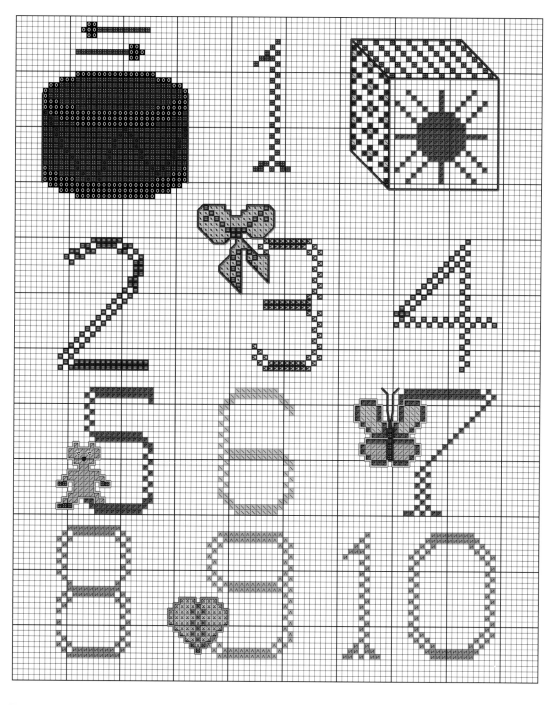

	DMC		DMC		DMC	Backstitch	French knots	
	898		791		702	— 898	🖤	310
	310		793		781	— 791	🖤	898
	349		550		783	— 741		
	608		741			— 781		
	972		700					

WORKING
THE CROSS STITCH

Cross stitch the border design inside each square, then find the centre and work the numbers and motifs as shown.

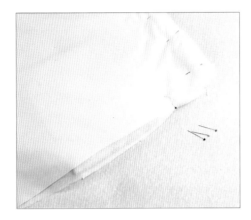

1 To make up: iron the interfacing to the wrong side. Lay the Anne fabric and lining down with right sides together. Lay the wadding (batting) on top and pin through all the layers.

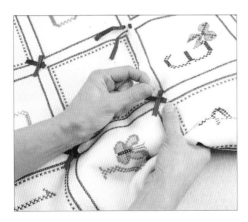

2 Stitch round the sides close to the cross stitch, leaving a small gap for turning. Trim the excess fabric, turn the quilt through and ease out the corners. Slip stitch the gap and press the seams gently. Attach a 15 cm (6 in) piece of ribbon at the corners of each square, sewing through all the layers to give a quilted effect. Sew or tie the ribbon into a small bow to finish.

BROOCH CUSHION

Keep your brooches safe by pinning them to this delicate cushion.

*two 20 cm (8 in) squares of
white 36 count evenweave linen*

tacking (basting) thread

needle

embroidery hoop (frame)

*stranded cotton DMC 221,
223, 224, 225, 501, 502, 503,
832, 834, 839, 3032, 3782*

tapestry needle

80 cm (32 in) wine piping

pins

sewing machine

sewing thread

scissors

20 cm (8 in) cushion pad

WORKING THE CROSS STITCH

Tack (baste) guidelines in both directions across the centre of the cross stitch panel. Work the cross stitch using a single strand of cotton over two threads of linen.

1 To make up: tack the piping round the edge of the embroidered panel, overlapping the ends of the piping at one corner. With right sides together, stitch round three sides of the cushion, close to the piping. Trim the seams and corners, then turn through. Press the cushion cover and insert the pad. Slip stitch the gap to finish.

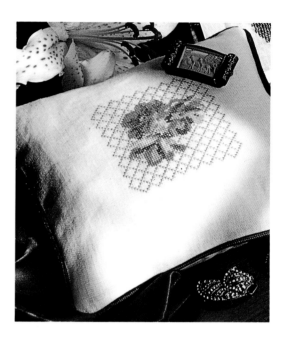

DMC	
-- -	501
11	502
1 1	503
■■	221
3 3	223
4 4	224
5 5	225
7 7	839
9 9	832
II II	834
◇◇	3032
✕✕	3782
☆	Middle point

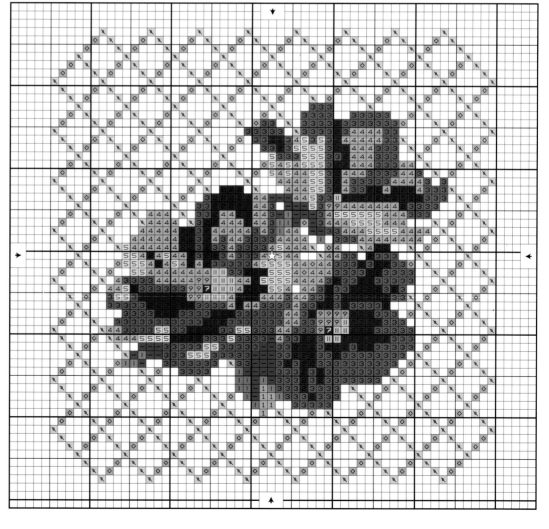

GREETINGS CARD

The card makes a present in itself for a special friend.

WORKING THE CROSS STITCH

Tack (baste) the fine calico to the back of the silk and fit into a hoop. Tack the waste canvas onto the middle of the fabric, keeping the canvas in line with the grain of the fabric. Mark the centre of the canvas. Stitch the design using two strands of cotton. When complete, fray and pull out the canvas threads one at a time. Press on the reverse side and trim to fit behind the opening.

YOU WILL NEED

20 cm (8 in) square of fine calico

20 cm (8 in) square of cream silk dupion (mid-weight silk)

tacking (basting) thread

needle

embroidery hoop (frame)

13 x 15 cm (5 x 6 in) 14 count waste canvas

stranded cotton DMC 221, 223, 224, 744, 3362, 3363

embroidery needle

scissors

craft card with an 8 x 12 cm (3 in x 4¾ in) aperture (opening)

double-sided tape

1 To make up: stick tape round the inside edge of the opening and position the embroidery on top. Stick the backing card in position. Use double-sided tape to assemble because glue tends to buckle the card.

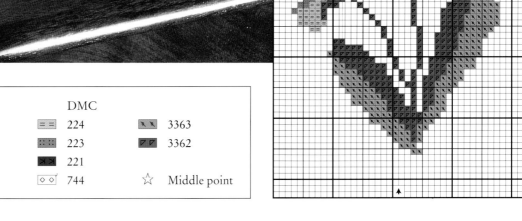

DMC		
══ 224	✗✗ 3363	
⋮⋮⋮ 223	◪◪ 3362	
◆◆ 221		
◇◇ 744	☆ Middle point	

HANDKERCHIEF CASE

No more scrabbling in the drawer, this pretty and practical pouch will keep all your hankies tidy.

YOU WILL NEED

two 53 x 20 cm (21 x 8 in) pieces of white 36 count evenweave linen

tacking (basting) thread

needle

embroidery hoop (frame)

stranded cotton DMC 221, 223, 224, 225, 501, 502, 503, 832, 834, 839, 3032, 3782

tapestry needle

pins

sewing machine

sewing thread

scissors

1 m (1 yd) wine coloured piping

WORKING THE CROSS STITCH

Tack (baste) a guideline crossways 10 cm (4 in) from one end of the linen. Mark the centre of this line and begin the cross stitch. The bottom of the design is the side nearest the raw edge.

Work the design using a single strand of cotton over two threads of linen. When the embroidery is complete, press on the reverse side. A magnifying glass might help.

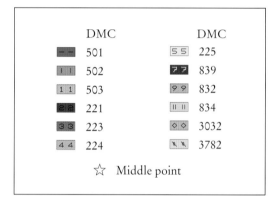

DMC	DMC
-- 501	55 225
11 502	77 839
11 503	99 832
22 221	II II 834
33 223	◇◇ 3032
44 224	⬂⬂ 3782
☆ Middle point	

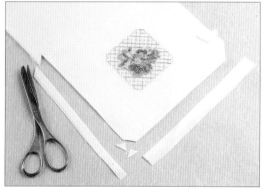

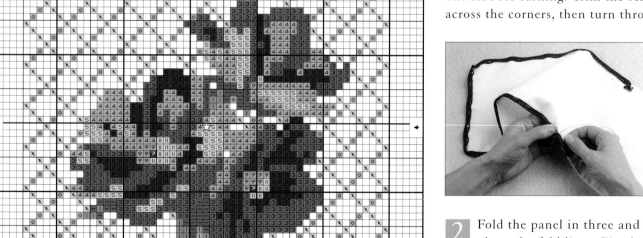

1 To make up: pin the two linen panels together with the embroidery to the inside. With a 2 cm (¾ in) seam allowance, sew all round leaving a gap on one side for turning. Trim the seams and across the corners, then turn through.

2 Fold the panel in three and tack along the fold lines. Pin the piping to the inside of the front flap and down both sides as far as the second fold line. Turn under the ends and slip stitch the piping in place. Slip stitch the side seams to complete the case.

BAND SAMPLER

Enjoy stitching these ornate and colourful bands, then select
your own initials to embroider at the bottom.

YOU WILL NEED

25 x 50 cm (10 x 20 in) cream
28 count Cashel linen, Zweigart
E3281

tacking (basting) thread

needle

rotating frame

stranded cotton DMC 224, 225,
312, 347, 3328, 3362, 3363,
3722

tapestry needle

30 x 50 cm (12 x 20 in) cream
cotton lawn

pins

sewing thread

scissors

two wooden hanging bars

50 cm (20 in) red cord

WORKING THE CROSS STITCH

Tack (baste) a guideline crossways, 8 cm (3 in) from one end of the linen. Begin 5 cm (2 in) in from the side and work down the chart using two strands of cotton over two threads. Select your own initials and stitch them at the bottom of the sampler. Press on the reverse side when complete.

1 To make up: pin the lining to the linen with the embroidery facing in and stitch down both sides close to the cross stitch. Trim the seams and turn through.

2 Press the panel and fold the ends over the wooden bars. Turn under a small hem and stitch securely. Tie the cord to the top bar and tuck the ends inside the hem.

DMC					
■	347	◆	312	╱	225
■	3362	＼	3363	＼	3328
＞	224	◤	3722	☆	Middle point

GIFT TAG

This gift tag would also look very pretty hanging
from the wardrobe door key.

YOU WILL NEED

8 cm (3 in) square of 18 count
Rustico, Zweigart E3292

stranded cotton DMC 500, 550,
552, 554, 3363, 3364, 3820

tapestry needle

15 cm (6 in) square of natural
handmade paper

craft knife

safety ruler

scissors

all-purpose glue

single hole punch

two reinforcing rings

DMC	
▤▤	552
⸪⸪⸪	554
⊁⊁	3820
◈◈	3363
⟍⟍	3364

Backstitch	
——	550
——	500

☆	Middle point

WORKING THE CROSS STITCH

Beginning in the centre of the canvas, work the
cross stitch design using two strands of cotton, and
the backstitch using a single strand.

1 To make up: cut two
tag shapes out of the
handmade paper, and with
the craft knife, cut an
opening in one. Stick the
embroidered panel in the
window and trim the edges
of the fabric. Glue the
back of the label in place.

2 Once the glue has
dried, punch a hole
at the end of the tag and
stick the reinforcing rings
on either side. Plait a
length of dark green, gold
and purple threads
together and loop through
the hole to finish the tag.

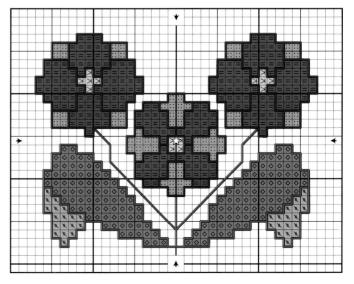

COTTAGE GARDEN TEA COSY

YOU WILL NEED

30 x 40 cm (12 x 16 in) antique white 28 count evenweave linen

tacking (basting) thread

needle

embroidery hoop (frame)

stranded cotton DMC 341, 352, 372, 422, 433, 435, 451, 543, 666, 725, 746, 776, 778, 825, 828, 899, 951, 986, 989, 3346, 3348, 3726, 3746, 3766, 3799, black

tapestry needle

scissors

30 x 40 cm (12 x 16 in) lining fabric

30 x 40 cm (12 x 16 in) wadding (batting)

pins

sewing machine

sewing thread

80 cm (32 in) cord

Traditional china teapots need a little help to keep the tea warm. This padded tea cosy is just the job.

WORKING THE CROSS STITCH

Tack (baste) guidelines across the centre of the linen in both directions and work the cross stitch using two strands of cotton over two threads. Work the paving slabs using two strands of 433 and all other backstitch using a single strand of cotton. The half cross stitch is also worked using a single strand of cotton (3348). Press on the reverse side when complete.

1 To make up: enlarge the template and cut out the front panel from embroidered linen. You will also need a back in linen, two lining pieces and two pieces of wadding. Put the embroidered linen and one piece of lining together with right sides facing and place the wadding on top. Pin the layers together along the straight edge, then tack and stitch. Repeat with the other pieces.

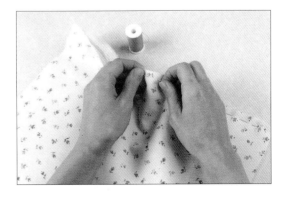

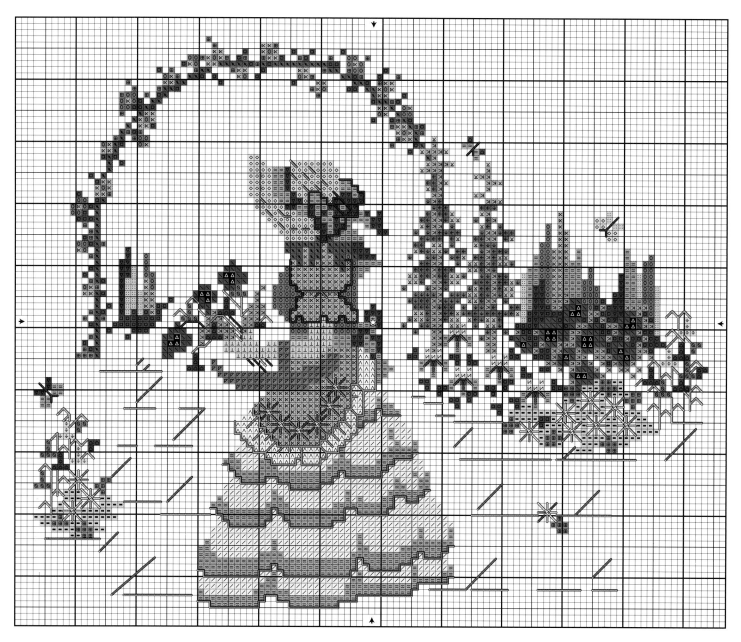

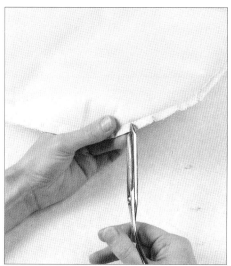

2 Turn the wadding to the inside, pin the panels, right sides facing, and stitch the curved edge. Trim, and notch the curves.

3 Turn through to the right side and press lightly. Slip stitch the cord in place, making a loop for a handle in the middle.

DMC			
≡ ≡	341	↓ ↓	3346
∴ ∴	352	← ←	3726
⊁ ⊁	372	▽ ▽	3746
◇ ◇	422	⊘ ⊘	3766
◣ ◣	433	▲ ▲	310
▽ ▽	435	▬ ▬	3348
∕ ∕	543		
■ ■	666		Backstitch
И И	725	——	451
∧ ∧	746	——	776
⊠ ⊠	776	——	3726
⊠ ⊠	778	——	3746
◤ ◤	825	——	989
÷ ÷	828	——	3799
○ ○	899	——	433
⊥ ⊥	951		
⊡ ⊡	986	☆	Middle point
⊞ ⊞	989		

PIN CUSHION

This design may look complicated, but it is easy if you work the floral design first and then fill in the tartan background.

YOU WILL NEED

20 cm (8 in) square of ivory 18 count Aida

tacking (basting) thread

needle

interlocking bar frame

stranded cotton Anchor 2, 43, 110, 112, 210, 226, 235, 268, 291, 337, 340, 403

tapestry needle

scissors

15 cm (6 in) square backing fabric

pins

sewing machine

sewing thread

polyester stuffing

40 cm (16 in) purple satin bias binding

WORKING THE CROSS STITCH

Tack (baste) guidelines across the centre of the Aida in both directions and work the cross stitch using a single strand of cotton. Once complete, press lightly on the reverse side and trim the seams to 5 mm (¼ in).

Anchor		◇◇	43		◥◥	112		✕✕	340
═ ═	2	✕✕	291	⫽⫽	268			
⁘⁘	226	◩◩	110	∧∧	337	☆	Middle point
▶▶	210	◢◢	403	✕✕	235		

1 To make up: with right sides facing outwards, stitch the backing to the embroidered panel close to the cross stitch, leaving a gap on one side. Use polyester stuffing to fill the pin cushion and backstitch the gap closed.

2 Open out one side of the binding and pin round the underside of the seam. Join the ends of the binding, then tack and sew in position. Fold the binding onto the right side and slip stitch close to the cross stitch to finish.

TABLE MAT

This versatile mat would look marvellous on any shape or size of table.
You could change the colour of the trellis
to match your own décor.

WORKING THE CROSS STITCH

Tack (baste) guidelines in both directions across the centre of the linen. Beginning in the centre, work one quarter of the design using two strands of Marlitt over three threads. Once complete, turn the fabric through 90 degrees and work the next section of the cross stitch. The design on each quarter is identical and is not a mirror image. Work the other section in the same way.

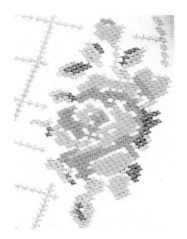

YOU WILL NEED

50 cm (20 in) square of white
36 count evenweave linen

tacking (basting) thread

needle

embroidery hoop (frame)

Anchor Marlitt 816,
852, 879, 897, 881

tapestry needle

scissors

sewing machine

sewing thread

1 To make up: once complete, press on the reverse side with a damp cloth. Trim the linen to 40 cm (16 in) diameter. Turn under a narrow hem and tack in position.

2 Stitch close to the folded edge, slip stitch the corners and tack in position. Press carefully as Marlitt is a synthetic thread and may be damaged by a hot iron.

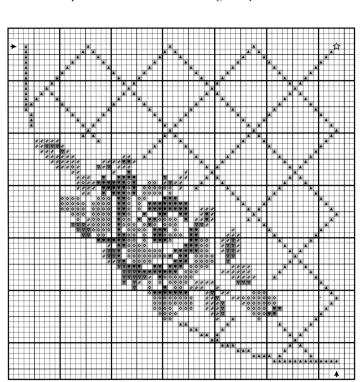

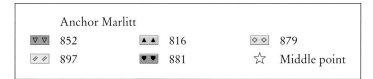

Anchor Marlitt

▽▽	852	▲▲	816	◇◇	879
⁄⁄	897	♥♥	881	☆	Middle point

SCHOOL SAMPLER

This nineteenth-century sampler is typical of those worked in schools by girls as young as nine or ten as part of their general education.

YOU WILL NEED

40 cm (16 in) square of cream 28 count Cashel linen, Zweigart E3281

tacking (basting) thread

needle

embroidery hoop (frame)

stranded cotton DMC 224, 301, 312, 347, 355, 356, 783, 3362, 3363

tapestry needle

scissors

40 cm (16 in) square of lightweight calico

30 cm (12 in) square of mount board (backing board)

strong thread

picture frame

WORKING THE CROSS STITCH

Tack (baste) guidelines in both directions across the centre of the linen. Work the cross stitch and back stitch using two strands of cotton over two threads of linen.

1 To make up: once complete, press on the reverse side. Lay the lightweight calico on top and then the mount board (backing board). Check the position of the embroidery and make sure the border is straight. Stretch over the mount board. Fit into a frame of your choice.

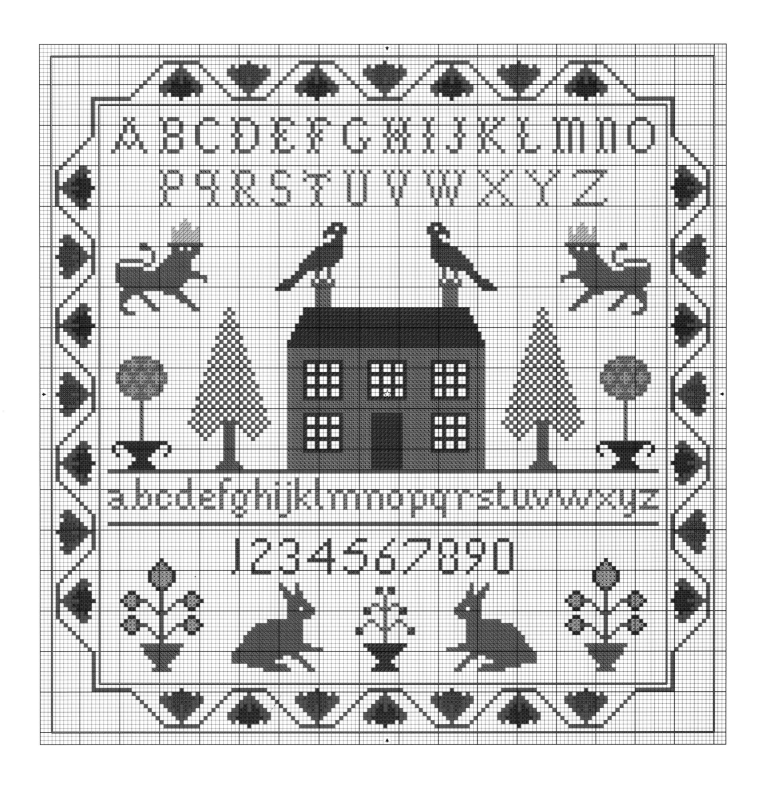

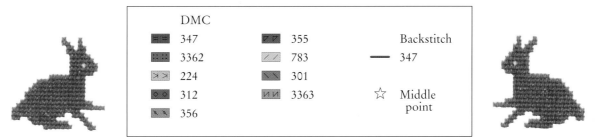

DMC				
347		355	Backstitch	
3362		783	347	
224		301		
312		3363	☆ Middle point	
356				

BIRTH KEEPSAKE

This pretty gift has a practical use as a pin cushion, but could be filled with lavender or potpourri instead.

YOU WILL NEED

15 cm (6 in) square of white 25 count Lugana, Zweigart E3835

tacking (basting) thread

needle

embroidery hoop (frame)

stranded cotton DMC 350, 472, 3326

tapestry needle

118 small pink beads

scissors

15 cm (6 in) square of white backing fabric

sewing machine

sewing thread

two 14 cm (5½ in) squares of wadding (batting)

pins

75 cm (30 in) white crocheted lace edging (dipped in weak tea to colour slightly)

WORKING THE CROSS STITCH

Tack (baste) guidelines in both directions across the centre of the linen. Work the cross stitch using three strands of cotton over two threads. Once complete, sew a bead over the top of each stitch in the pink hearts. Use a double length of thread and begin with a secure knot.

	DMC		
▽ ▽	350	☆	Middle
▲ ▲	472		point
◆ ◆	3326		

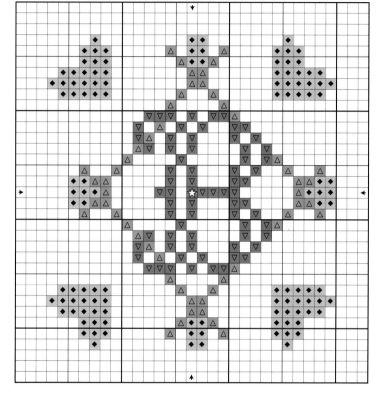

1 To make up: block the design if necessary and trim away the excess fabric leaving 4 cm (1½ in) round the cross stitch. Cut the backing fabric to match and stitch the embroidery and backing fabric together with right sides facing, leaving a gap along one side. Trim the seams and across the corners.

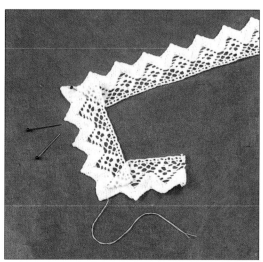

2 Tuck the wadding (batting) into the cushion and slip stitch to close. Mitre the corners of the lace one at a time by folding and stitching diagonally on the wrong side. Each side should be about 13 cm (5 in) long. Join the lace ends and pin round the cushion 1 cm (³⁄₈ in) in from the edge. Stitch in place.

SEWING BOX

The lid of this box has an inset to fit the padded top and can be stained or painted to suit.

YOU WILL NEED

15 cm (6 in) square of cream 22 count Hardanger

tacking (basting) thread

needle

embroidery hoop (frame)

stranded cotton DMC 725, 726, 783, 3362, 3363, 3364, 3687, 3688, 3689

tapestry needle

11.5 cm (4½ in) blank wooden box

oak woodstain

antique wax

compass cutter

10 cm (4 in) square of mount board (backing board)

scissors

sewing thread

10 cm (4 in) square of foam rubber

all-purpose glue

WORKING THE CROSS STITCH

Tack (baste) guidelines in both directions across the centre of the Hardanger and work the cross stitch using a single strand of cotton over one pair of threads. Stain the wooden box and finish with several coats of wax.

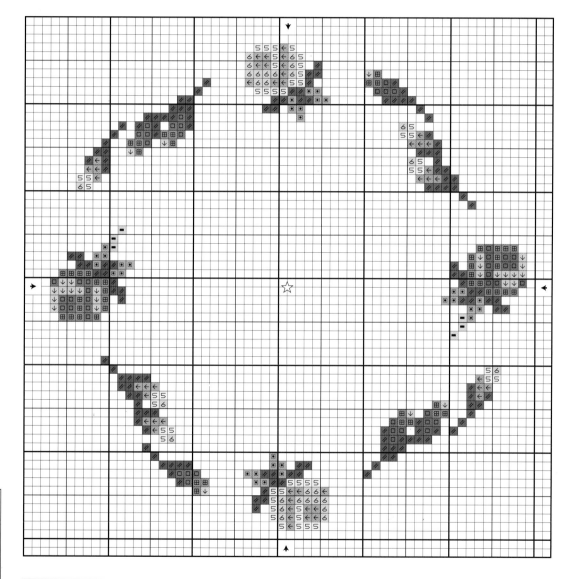

	DMC
5 5	725
6 6	726
⬚⬚	3687
⊞⊞	3688
↓↓	3689
←←	783
▬▬	3364
⊡⊡	3363
▨▨	3362
☆	Middle point

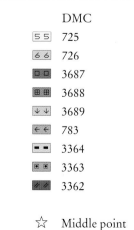

1 To make up: measure the diameter of the inset and cut the mount board (backing board) and foam to fit inside. Keeping the embroidery in the centre, cut the Hardanger 2 cm (¾ in) larger and work a row of small running stitches round the edge.

2 Give the embroidered Hardanger a final press before positioning the fabric face down with the foam and then the mount board (backing board) disc on top of it. Pull up the gathers, check the embroidery is central and stitch the ends securely. Stick in position on the box lid.

TRADITIONAL CHRISTMAS STOCKING

Hang this beautiful brocade stocking on the fireplace and who knows what Santa might bring?

YOU WILL NEED

50 cm (20 in) of 10 cm wide bleached linen band, Inglestone collection 900/100

tacking (basting) thread

needle

tapestry needle

fine gold braid Kreinik 102

stranded cotton DMC 99, 3052, 3802

blending filament Kreinik 045, 093

scissors

45 x 60 cm (18 x 24 in) pink and cream floral brocade

38 x 60 cm (15 x 24 in) lining

pins

sewing machine

sewing thread

WORKING THE CROSS STITCH

Tack (baste) guidelines across the linen band as shown and stitch a motif in each space, staggering them diagonally. Work the cross stitch using three strands of cotton over two threads of linen. Add a strand of blending filament with the green and pink threads before stitching.

	DMC
◇ ◇	Kreinik fine braid gold 102
▦ ▦	3052 + Blending filament 045
= =	99 + Blending filament 093
▶ ▶	3802
☆	Middle point

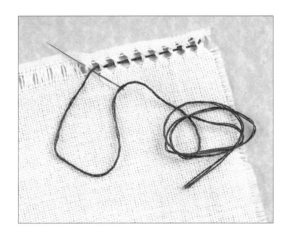

1 To make up: draw out seven threads near the top and bottom edge of the linen band. Using three strands of 3802, twist groups of three threads as shown to make a decorative border.

2 Scale up the template and cut two pieces each out of brocade and lining. With 2 cm (³⁄₄ in) seam allowances, stitch the lining pieces together with right sides facing. Trim the seams and snip into the curves. Make the stocking in the same way but with a 1.5 cm (⁵⁄₈ in) seam allowance. Turn through and fold the top edge over 5 cm (2 in).

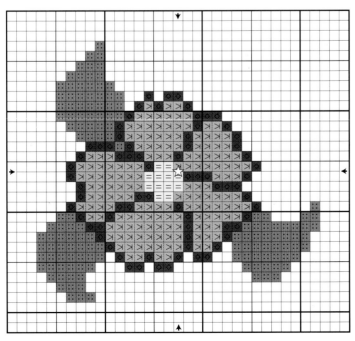

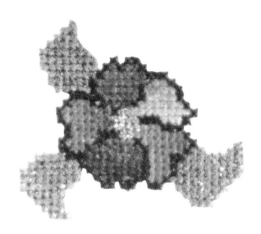

3 Make a tab using a piece of brocade 8 x 20 cm (3 x 8 in). Fold lengthways and stitch, then turn through and press with the seam in the middle of the reverse side. Fold the tab in half and pin onto the back seam of the stocking and sew securely. Fold over 1 cm ($^3/_8$ in) at the top of the lining and tuck inside the stocking. Pin and tack in position 5 cm (2 in) down from the top and slip stitch. Pin the cuff round the top of the stocking. Slip stitch the back seam and use running stitch to secure the cuff to the stocking.

NEEDLEWORK TIP

Make a small version of the stocking in evenweave linen with a single motif stitched on the front.

CHRISTMAS DECORATIONS

These Victorian toys are quick and easy to sew on this special vinyl canvas which has a similar weave to Hardanger.

YOU WILL NEED

20 cm (8 in) square of 14 count vinyl weave canvas

stranded cotton Anchor white, 46, 134, 399, 778

fine gold braid Kreinik 002

tapestry needle

scissors

20 cm (8 in) square of thin gold card (cardboard)

all-purpose glue

WORKING THE CROSS STITCH

Stitch the designs onto the canvas using three strands of cotton or the fine gold braid as it comes.

1 To make up: cut round the edge, leaving one row of canvas showing. Oversew the edges with gold braid, except for the rocker on the horse which is oversewn with three strands of blue stranded cotton.

2 Sew a loop of braid onto the saddle, one onto the helmet and one in the middle of the top edge of the drum.

3 Draw round each decoration onto the card (cardboard). Cut out inside the lines and stick the card onto the back of the decoration. Trim away any excess card which is visible on the right side.

Anchor		134	Kreinik
399		778	fine braid gold 002
white		46	

CHRISTMAS CARDS

These snowflakes could be mounted back to back in a card ring to make an unusual tree decoration.

WORKING THE CROSS STITCH

Tack (baste) the calico onto the back of the fabric and fit into a small embroidery hoop (frame). Tack guidelines across the fabric to divide it into six equal segments. Mark the centre of one strip of canvas and tack onto the fabric, matching the centres and the guidelines.

	Anchor		Kreinik fine silver
= =	white	:::::	braid 001

1 To make up: work one of the cross stitch designs using two strands of cotton or the fine braid as it comes. Note that the centre stitch is omitted at this stage and sewn later. Once complete, remove the waste canvas carefully, one thread at a time.

2 Repeat the same design on each of the other guidelines to complete the snowflake. Once all the waste canvas is carefully removed, stitch the centre cross.

3 Remove from the frame, trim to size and stick behind the opening of the card. Stick the flap down to finish. Make another card stitching the other snowflake design onto a different fabric.

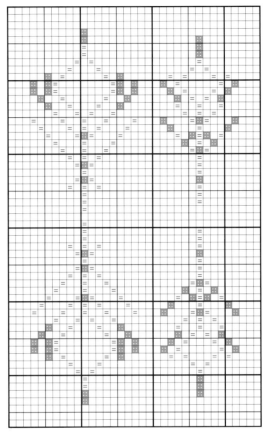

YOU WILL NEED

15 cm (6 in) square of silk dupion (mid-weight silk) or panné velvet

15 cm (6 in) square of fine calico

tacking (basting) thread

needle

flexihoop (small embroidery frame)

three 5 x 13 cm (2 x 5 in) strips of 14 count waste canvas

vanishing marker pen

tapestry needle

white stranded cotton

fine silver braid Kreinik 001

silver blending filament Kreinik 001 (optional)

scissors

greetings card with a 9.5 cm (3¾ in) diameter aperture (opening)

double-sided tape

CHRISTMAS WREATH PICTURE

TRADITIONAL

Make a fresh holly wreath and decorate with red and orange berries
to complement the colours in this embroidery.

YOU WILL NEED

36 cm (14 in) square of cream
14 count Aida

tacking (basting) thread

needle

embroidery hoop (frame)

stranded cotton Anchor white,
47, 214, 228, 236, 313,
314, 1041

tapestry needle

scissors

sewing thread

24 cm (9½ in) diameter
mount board (backing board)

WORKING THE CROSS STITCH

Tack (baste) guidelines in both directions across the centre of the Aida and work the cross stitch design using two strands of cotton. Press on the reverse side when complete.

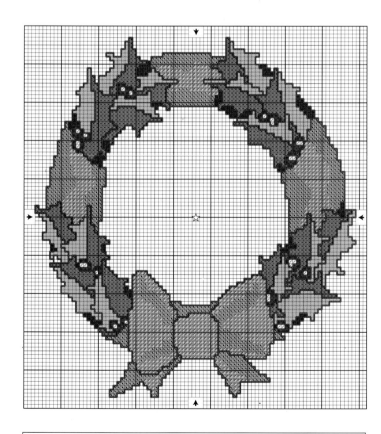

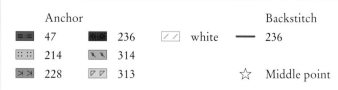

Anchor			Backstitch
47	236	⁄⁄ white	— 236
214	314		
228	313		☆ Middle point

1 To make up: trim the Aida to make a 30 cm (12 in) circle with the embroidery in the middle. Using a double thread, sew a row of running stitches round the outside edge. Place the mount board (backing board) on the reverse side and pull up the gathers.

2 Check that the embroidery is straight and central on the mount board then sew in the ends securely. Mount in a picture frame of your choice. Alternatively you could make a fresh wreath on a standard wire frame and attach it to the embroidery with very fine florist's wire.

ANGEL PICTURE

Hang this serene angel above the fireplace at Christmas time and decorate the tree with matching baubles.

YOU WILL NEED

*20 x 25 cm (8 x 10 in) ivory
18 count Aida*

tacking (basting) thread

needle

interlocking bar frame

tapestry needle

*stranded cotton Anchor white,
94, 127, 136, 150, 298, 380,
881, 889, 894, 897, 970*

scissors

*14.5 x 17.5 cm (5¾ x 6¾ in)
mount board (backing board)*

strong thread

picture frame

WORKING THE CROSS STITCH

Tack (baste) guidelines in both directions across the centre of the Aida and work the cross stitch using two strands of cotton. Work the backstitch to finish.

1 To make up: press on the reverse side and stretch over the mount board (backing board). Fit into a suitably festive frame of your choice.

Anchor		
– – white	◇ ◇	894
╱ ╱ 94	⊠ ⊠	970/894
═ ═ 127	⣿⣿	970
▽ ▽ 136	◪ ◪	897
◤ ◤ 150		
◺ ◺ 298	.	Backstitch
9 9 380	—	380
∧ ∧ 881		
⊠ ⊠ 889	☆	Middle point

TEMPLATES

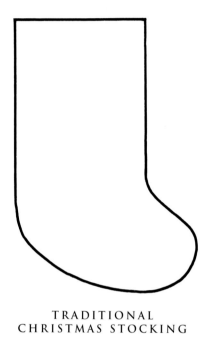

TRADITIONAL
CHRISTMAS STOCKING

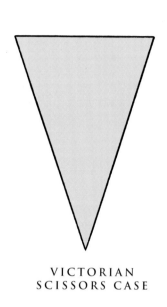

VICTORIAN
SCISSORS CASE

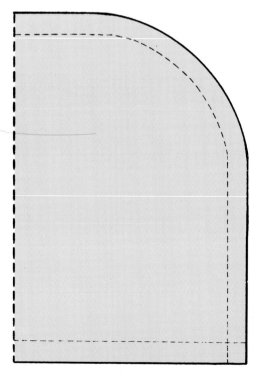

COTTAGE GARDEN
TEA COSY

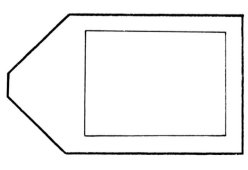

GIFT TAG